DAGGABURRA STATE SCHOOL
Poetry Study Unit
Ms. Kranke's Year 6 Class

TROY THOMPSON'S

This year we will be writing our own beautiful poems. Sadly, many people think that reading and writing poetry is silly and a waste of time. These people do not understand what poetry really is and what it can do for them.

EXCELLENT

Some poets believe that the ideas for their poetry are "inspired." The word "inspire" comes from the prefix "in" meaning "into," and the Latin word "spirare" meaning "to breathe," so sometimes poets feel that their writing is "breathed into" them from a very moving life experience.

~~PROET~~ PEOTRY

In our poetry study unit we will be learning to WRITE OUR OWN POEMS. Ideas for each type of poem that you will be asked to write will be suggested to you as part of an ASSIGNMENT.

BOOK

Paste each assignment sheet in your SPECIAL POETRY EXERCISE BOOK, and WRITE YOUR POEM beneath it. If your poetry is very good, it will be entered in the Farmers' Auxiliary (inc. Bull Breeders' Association) POETRY CONTEST at the end of the year. The winner will receive a COMPUTER, and the school will receive $500 WORTH OF SOFTWARE of the winner's choice. So remember our school motto and always "TRY HARDER."

Ms. Kranke

A lot of this was written by Gary Crew and put together by Craig Smith

CHILDREN
TRAFFIC ISLAND
PLAY GROUND
STEEP DESCENT
STEEP CLIMB
GRID
GATE
HILL
CREST
GRAVEL ROAD
DIP
TRAM
STOP SIGN AHEAD

Kane/Miller Book Publishers

POETRY ASSIGNMENT I

Nobody really knows when people first began writing poetry, but we do know that the oldest surviving poems were usually about events that could not be explained. Often these poems are about terrible disasters (such as the floods in the "Epic of Gilgamesh" from Ancient Sumer) or even fearful and mythical animals (such as the giant Roc in "Sinuhe the Sailor" from Ancient Egypt, or another giant bird, the Garuda, from Ancient India). The stories of these creatures and events were written in verse and often told by wandering poets who would recite their poems in a royal court or even a marketplace.

Your assignment is to write a poem telling the story of a fearful event or creature as if you were one of these ancient poets. Your purpose might be to praise a popular hero who slew a monster or saved a town. Whatever you choose, it should entertain your audience with a wonderful, mythical tale.

Early poetry often rhymed so that it sounded more musical. The use of rhyme also made the poem easier to remember if it had to be told "by heart." Your poem can rhyme if you like, but it does not have to.

A poem of at least six verses is expected. Each verse should have a minimum of four lines. You should give your poem a title. You might even like to add a drawing to make your poem more exciting.

Remember our contest, and keep your work NEAT!

Ms. Kranke

cranky
spanky
bogie
logie
(old) fogie
wee
pee
plop
slop

bum
numb
dumb
scum
crumb
mum
dad
bad
sad
mad

poop
loop
spew
stew
snot
clot
pot
bot

crap
clap
slap
spit
hit

You have made the mythical beast
"come alive" through your words.
I found myself gripped in panic and
excitement by the cave peoples' plight.
Who needs Steven Spielberg?

7/10 Ms. Kranke

The Attack of the Killer Sabre Tooth or How Troy Thompson saved the Cave People

A long time ago when the world was dark
A sabre tooth lived in Jurassic Park.
It ate little boys, it chomped little goils,
It especially liked babies whose hair was in coils.

Not one of the cave people knew what to do,
When they spotted that tiger they'd always shoot thru.
Their clubs were no use and nor were their spears
And night after night they dreamed of their fears.

But one morning a hero came into their cave,
His name was Troy Thompson, their lives he would save.
His body was muscly, his brain was no feather
And he brought his two dogs who were tougher than leather.

"Oh Troy, Troy." all the people did cry
"Will you save us today or we will all die."
"No sweat," answered Troy, "you've asked the right'dood',
We'll get rid of the tiger but first give us food."

And so after dinner Troy hid in the bush
(In the cave not a person would even say "Shush")
And just as the dark-time came falling down fast
That tiger came prowling, 'twas the meanest and last.

But Troy wasn't frightened, oh no, not a bit.
He leapt out and gave it a Kung-Fu King-Hit.
When all of the cave people heard of this act,
They called Troy a legend and that is a fact.

POETRY ASSIGNMENT II

A form of poetry known as "Haiku" has been a tradition among the Japanese people for thousands of years. Haiku is a delicate method of expression. Its form has a few simple rules: (1) The poem has only three lines. (2) The first line has five syllables, the second, seven, the third, five. (3) The poem should not rhyme. (4) Overall, the poem should "paint a little picture in words." (5) Haiku poems usually do not have a title.

Sorry, Miss Ms. Kranke.
I tried to "paint a little picture in words" —
but I spilt the paint!

Here is an example of a haiku:

> *Eyes ever watchful,*
> *Body in silent motion,*
> *She swoops on her prey.*

What picture have you formed in your mind after reading this?

For this assignment you will need to write three Haiku of your own:(1) Based on an animal that you admire. (2) Based on an element of your local environment which you especially like. (3) Your own special or secret place.

Ms. Kranke

Very gentle and lyrical, Troy, — who would have thought you had it in you? (Notwithstanding the "P" word).

I'm flattered! (I think!)

9/10 Ms Kranke

AN ANIMAL I ADMIRE. I like two animals. They are my dogs, Ferris and Bueller. I named them after my favorite video, "Ferris Bueller's Day Off." It's about this cool (dood) who takes a day off school with his girlfriend (a girl) and his best friend (a boy). My dog called Ferris is a Jack Russell terrier. He is a boy dog. He is very small and (tuff.) His color is tan and white. Bueller is a girl. She is a humongous black dog. She is half Rottweiler and half Doberman. She is very gentle. But can be tough.

Here is my Haiku about my dogs.

Tongues wet and licky,

Tails that wag when I come home.

They poop in the park.

A GOOD PLACE IN MY ENVIRONMENT. I like the park down the road. I take Ferris and Bueller for walks there. My friends say I should have called the dogs Arnie and Danny after Arnie Schwarzenegger and Danny DeVito who were in an excellent video called "Twins." (They REALLY WERE twins but Arnie was big and muscly and Danny was short and fat). The park is an excellent place. I ride my bike and meet my friends there. Sometimes I skateboard or rollerblade there. There is a concrete bike path through the park but old ladies like to walk on it and that sometimes causes trouble.

Here is my Haiku about the park.

Wide and green and flat,

Grass as soft as spongy mat.

It feels nice on feet.

A SECRET PLACE. This is the hardest thing to write about because it means that I have to give away a secret. But since I don't think you would like my secret place, Ms. Kranke, I have done what you asked me. I have really had to "TRY HARDER" because I don't like giving away secrets. My secret place is the old outhouse in our backyard. When I have had a bad day and need to be by myself I go down there to sit and think.

Here is my Haiku about the old outhouse.

It's dark and quiet.

Cobwebs hang from the tin roof.

The world is outside.

POETRY ASSIGNMENT III

Another very early form of poetry is called the ballad. The ballad usually tells the story of a noble hero who meets with tragedy. Listening to a ballad is like imagining all the scenes from a film in your head, where each verse is like a separate scene in the overall action.

Ballads often repeat lines to stress an important part of the action, or even the particular feelings that the poet wants to arouse in the listener. Ballads may include some of the actual speech of the hero or villain, and they often rhyme.

My own favorite ballad is called "Lord Lovel." It is about a young knight who leaves his love, Lady Nancy, to go roving, promising to marry her on his return. Sadly, the very day he came back, Lady Nancy died:

> So he order'd the grave to be open'd wide,
> And the shroud he turned down,
> And there he kiss'd her clay-cold lips,
> Till the tears came trickling down.

> Lady Nancy she died, as it might be, today,
> Lord Lovel he died as tomorrow;
> Lady Nancy she died out of pure, pure grief,
> Lord Lovel he died out of sorrow.

All night, I admit I don't look my best in the morning! Ms. Kranke

Lord Lovel and Lady Nancy died from broken hearts. I think that's very sad, don't you?

In this assignment you are required to choose an exciting episode from history that you can retell as a ballad. Remember that your poem should have a noble hero who loses his or her life for a good cause.

Ms. Kranke

Kylie dear, they'll not find us here

R.I.P TROY CASSANOVA THOMPSON

Poor Kylie! Ms. Kranke

THE BALLAD OF SERGEANT THOMPSON.

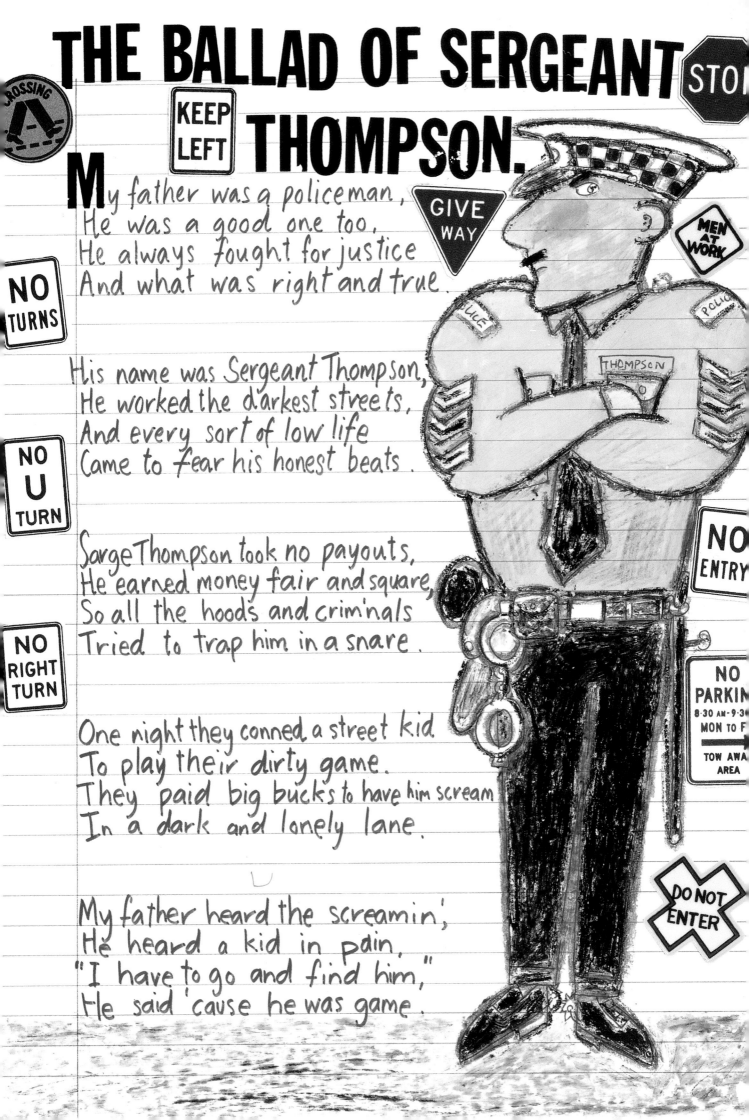

My father was a policeman,
He was a good one too,
He always fought for justice
And what was right and true.

His name was Sergeant Thompson,
He worked the darkest streets,
And every sort of low life
Came to fear his honest beats.

Sarge Thompson took no payouts,
He earned money fair and square,
So all the hoods and crimi'nals
Tried to trap him in a snare.

One night they conned a street kid
To play their dirty game.
They paid big bucks to have him scream
In a dark and lonely lane.

My father heard the screamin',
He heard a kid in pain,
"I have to go and find him,"
He said 'cause he was game.

But that alley it was lonely,
That alley it was dark,
And when my dad had entered,
He saw a cigarette spark.

He saw the kid he thought was hurt
Just leanin' on a bin,
And as he drew back on his smoke,
He screamed a bogus din.

"I have been tricked," my father said,
But then his voice was smothered
'Cause before he said another word,
The low life had him covered.

ONE WAY

Sarge Thompson didn't stand a chance,
(Street scum are never slow),
They fired once, they fired twice,
And his blood began to flow.

And so he died right there and then,
The darkness all around,
But I'm pretty sure he thought of me
As he was heaven bound.

by Troy Thompson

Dear Troy, your poem is very
moving. Your father is very lucky
to be remembered by you in this
way. Your father's death was
a very nasty business and I don't
want you to know the findings
necessarily agree with the findings
of the inquiry into the reason
your father was in the lane
that night.
Ms. Kranke 9½/10

"Dad" (1956-90) by Troy Thompson

(Ms. Kranke, the things that I have
told you in this poem really happened to my
dad so I would like it if you didn't read it aloud to the
class because it is very personal. Thank you T.T.)

POETRY ASSIGNMENT IV

I once had a mother called "mum",
Who grew a giiiinormous tum,
I thought it was a blister,
It was really my sister,
Who grew up to be a bass drum.

So far we have been writing very serious poetry. Now let's try some that are more fun.
The limerick is a little poem of only five lines, and it's always rather silly nonsense
that makes fun of someone. The rules for writing a limerick might seem complicated,
but once you get into the rhythm, you will find that they're quite easy. To write a
limerick you should remember that:

I once had a dad called "father"
Who every morning would get into bother
He would slice himself shaving
while he was raving
Instead of looking out for his lather.

* The first, second and fifth line rhyme.

* The third and fourth line rhyme.

* The first, second and fifth line have the same number of syllables and beats.

* The third and fourth lines have the same number of syllables and beats.

Here is a silly limerick that I wrote myself:

There was an old teacher called Kranke,
Who always went out with a hankie,
When she was asked why,
She would never reply,
That tearful old teacher called Kranke.

We had a Head master called Herman
Who was very excited by learnin

Your assignment is to write a limerick (more, if you like) about someone famous.

He loved stories about Monsters
especially the Munsters
And was always laughing
But his stories were
Ms. Kranke
his head off
very disturbin.

When I think of all
the subjects you may have
written about - bottoms, poo, nude smells etc,
I'm just glad you - Langley - spared my
feelings. For that alone I'm marking
you 10, in gratitude!
Ms. Kranke

There was a Super hero called Troy
Who was a most remarkable boy
He could play electric guitars
at night clubs and bars
and fly to Mars
with the other superstars

There was a pigeon called Ted
Who spent time in my bed
The cat put him there
And bits on the chair
Poor Ted was dead

There was a teacher
who always had a
To wipe tears from
when she saw Troy in
Because she thought he was just dandy
called "Barbie"
hankie handy
her eyes
disguise

Here are my limericks. I know that my dogs Ferris and Bueller aren't really famous, but I thought that if I wrote poetry about them, they might become famous when I do. My third limerick is about Michael Jackson. I like reading about him in "Who" Magazine. It's better than reading comics, I reckon.

There was a cute puppy

There was a cute puppy called Ferris
Who spent most of his life on a terrace,
But when the postman went by
He'd always give it a try
To bite him way down on his rear- ass.

There was a huge dog

There was a huge dog named Bueller
Whose guts became fuller and fuller
Until one dark nite
She took her last bite
And turned herself into a g'rilla.

There was a cool singer

There was a cool singer called Jackson
Whose moon walk was quite an attraction,
But one night as he danced
He got ants in his pants
And ended up strung up in traction.

POETRY ASSIGNMENT V

Many song lyrics are really poems set to music. You would know some of these - for example, "The Wild Colonial Boy" which is really a ballad sung to the tune of a traditional song. In this assignment we are going to write the words of a poem that could be set to song. To do this we will all use the tune of an old hymn that you used to sing in school, "Amazing Grace." It is a tune that can arouse deep emotions in the singer, so we will be writing a poem that suits that mood. Perhaps your poem could be dedicated to a person that you love? Try humming the tune of "Amazing Grace" to yourself as you write the words of your poem. You need only submit two verses.

Ms. Kranke

Hymn to Kylie
by Troy Thompson

(To be sung to the tune of "Amazing Grace."
Complete with instructions for emotional singing)

I love her - er-er bod
A-maz-in-in-ing grace
It is   so   cool
How sweet the sound
It cur-er-er-er-ves
That saved a wretch
Like-a wave
Like me
When I hold her-er-er hand
I once was lost   but
I get a shock
But now I'm found
Like a bolt o-o-of light-en-ing
Was blind but now I see

(Second verse, same as the first)

Her name i-i-i-is
Kyl-ie you know
She is my-i-i
Gir-l fr-iend
She-e makes Elle McP
Look like a witch
And that's good for my e-e-go.

But if I-i-i try
To come on strong
She socks me-e-e
In the teeth
Now I like a-a girl
Who knows her mind
But that's be-e-e-neath the belt.

So bo-y-y-ys
Treat your girls aw-right,
Like knights
O-o-of old use-d to,
O-or else you'll
End up in the poop,
Like me o-o-on Sat'dee nite

I'm very pleased to see you going through the "Art" section in the library for your reference, Troy. But I'm a bit concerned about what Kylie thinks of this! Perhaps paint bathing suit on top? Please, Troy? Ms. Kranke

My illustration is based on (well, photocopied really) the "Birth of Venus" by Botticelli (above) and "The Creation of Adam" by Michelangelo (left)

POETRY ASSIGNMENT VI

Another old form of poetry is the sonnet. There is more than one form of sonnet but all have 14 lines. The form that we will try to write is the Shakespearean sonnet, named after William Shakespeare, the great playwright. Shakespeare wrote "Romeo and Juliet"(you might have seen the film version starring Leonardo DiCaprio). But Shakespeare also wrote many beautiful sonnets, especially on the topics of love and growing old. I will read some of my favorites to you. Shakespeare used a special rhyme form in his sonnets. Line one rhymes with line three, line two with line four, line five with line seven, line six with line eight, and so on until the last two lines (13 and 14) rhyme to form what is called a "couplet."

Here is the rhyme scheme: **a b a b / c d c d / e f e f / g g.**

Your assignment is (1) to write two to three lines on the sonnet which you like the best from those I have read to you and (2) write a sonnet of your own on a meaningful topic.

Ms. Kranke

PART (1) Ms. Kranke, the sonnet that I liked best out of the ones you read in school was called "Death Be Not Proud" by the poet John Donne.

The part I liked best was the first part. I copied it out of a book in the library.

It went like this:

"Death, be not proud, though some have called thee
Mighty and dreadful, for thou art not so:
For those whom thou think'st thou dost overthrow
Die not, poor Death; nor yet canst thou kill me."

I can understand this poem because even if my father is dead he was a hero and is still alive in my memory. So I don't think the last line is really about me but my father. It is a good poem because it made me think.

Part (2) My own sonnet by Troy Thompson

WHEN I GROW UP

When I grow up I would like to be   (a)
A cop just like my dad,   (b)
And when I am, the crims will see   (a)
That I'll never do anything bad.   (b)
I will always wear a bullet-proof vest   (c)
So they can't gun me down.   (d)
Though they try their best I'll stand the test (c)
And they'll end up out of town.   (d)
So Dad, if you can hear me,   (e)
Wherever you're listening from,   (f)
Remember that it's not hard to be   (e)
Your proud and loving son.   (f)(sort of)
And Dad, although you're far away, you'd probably like to know (g)
That whatever I do and wherever I go, you're still my dad, the hero. (g)

Handwritten note: You've written a poem with real feeling. I was very moved and had a little cry. I'm sure you would make a fine policeman, but I fear if you don't start growing soon, you'll be defeated by the height requirement. Well done. Ms. Kranke 9½/10 ✓

POETRY ASSIGNMENT VII

Sometimes poets are asked to write a poem for a special occasion, such as the crowning of a king or queen. We have special occasions at school too - our prize giving night at the end of the year, for example, when your parents and friends come to see which students have been the best in their studies or even at sport or athletics.

Your assignment is to write "An Occasional Poem" which could be read aloud to the entire school, including parents, staff and visiting dignitaries. Sometimes even the Minister for Education might attend. What would you want to tell these people about your school on such an occasion?

Ms. Kranke

These pictures were done by my cousin Babette from an original idea by Troy Thompson
✓ You're both very clever. Ms. Kranke

An Oca Occasional Poem for Awards Night

I am a student of Daggaburra school,
It is like "outta sight,"
But there is one thing that isn't good
And y'all need to set it right.

The boys' toilets are all smelly,
The urinals smell like Mace,
When ever I need to go there,
I have to cover my face.

Mrs Ms. Kranke, that's my teacher,
(She is a good one too),
She lectures us on hygiene
But there's no soap in the loo!

So all you Big Knobs listening,
Spare a thought for us mid-terms,
'Cause when we go to take a pee
We only feed the germs.

-end-

Written and spoken by Troy
Thompson on behalf of the boys
(and girls, I guess) of the Daggaburra
Primary School. Authorized by the
Student Council. President, Kylie
Dragg.

From what I hear, the male staff
the boys toilet and the male staff
toilet are barely distinguishable.
With your permission I'll forward
this poem to the School
Council.
9/10 Ms. Kranke

POETRY ASSIGNMENT VIII

"Shape" or "concrete" poetry is a very interesting form of expression which is fun to try. For this assignment, try having the words of your poem fit the shape of the object which you are writing about. This type of poem can result in very dramatic effects.

Here is a "shape" poem I wrote myself. A clue to the poem is upside down at the top of the page...

Ms. Kranke

elePhants spell trouble for trees

My first go at shape poems - "Miss Krankeeee" and "Freedom."

miss Kranke eeeee

You could call a skateboard an escapeboard because it can take your mind off anything getting at you

I am hopeful of retaining at least some mystery in my life, Troy, so strictly speaking, I would prefer your poem "miss Krankeeee" to read "Ms. Krankeeee". This poem possibly uses too many drawn lines, rather than words, and even then makes me look - well - not a pretty sight. "Freedom" is very nice. Maybe I should take the skateboard poem "Freedom" & should take it up.

Ms. Kranke

My shape poem called "Two Bullets" by Troy Thompson

A bullet of deadly steel
One shot
blasted the target—a cop

along the dim alley littered with bottles
Another
blind blast seeks its prey and finds it.

My shape poem entitled

DEAD HI-TOPS by Troy Thompson

This poem uses "pop-up" technology,
but it doesn't always work

You're done an absolutely excellent job on your presentation, Troy. It is wonderful to see you using a computer in this artistic way, instead of those silly shooting games. Perhaps we might be able to find some time to examine the mechanics of "Pop-Up." Now, I suppose this is one of those fashionable "grungy" poems. Even so, you've written about things I'd rather not know about this. In spite of this, well done. — Mrs. Kraenke 8/10

with my

through the sew

even come near me until T

my mum's washing **MACHIN**

put sheets in with them and **I GO**

a week but that wasn't so bad beca

van daame video I watched them

My   old
hi-tops stink real
bad and if i take them
off after i've been down the park
dogs ferris and bueller or running
age outlet then my (gril) kylie wont
Hey're washed once i put them in
E and she **DIDN'T SEE** them and
T IN THE poop i was grounded for
use i got kylie to get me out every
back to back for a week excellent

POETRY ASSIGNMENT IX

The ode is a poem written as an expression of praise. The ode might praise anything admired by the poet - from another person, an animal, or an object of beauty. One poet, Alexander Pope, even wrote an ode in praise of solitude! But since some of the poems you have handed in lately have been so depressing, let's all TRY HARDER this time to write a really bright and happy ode in praise of someone - or something - really special!

I think that life can be short and lonely enough without spending all our time thinking miserable thoughts, don't you?

Ms. Kranke ★ Ideas for Odes

★ Ode to football. ★ Ode to basketball.

★ Ode to television.

★ Ode to Ferris and Bueller.

★ Ode to Kylie.

★ Ode to fish and chips. ★ Ode to milkshakes.

★ Ode to fishing and snorkeling when we go to the shack on holidays, and sometimes our neighbors Barry and Sandra take me out to the reef in their Haines Hunter and we go crabbing.

★ Ode to being left alone on Saturday mornings before football to get my thoughts together.

★ Ode to not doing the dishes. Or the vacuuming.

★ Ode to comics. ★ Ode to me. Ode to Ren and Stimpy.

★ Ode to the Royal Show ★ Ode to other odes.

★ Ode to elephants. Ode to Royce's (my brother) motorcycle.

POETRY ASSIGNMENT X

So far we have attempted some very complex poetic forms, and most of you have handled them very well. Now it's time that you had some more fun.

Our next assignment is to write an acrostic poem. Here is an example of one that I have written myself - about myself.

Mostly found in her school room
She likes to be with her students

Kind to all small creatures
Rarely angry
Always smiling
Never unfair or unreasonable
Knitting is her favorite pastime
Except when she's marking students' assignments.

Now try an acrostic poem for yourself - and about yourself!

Ms. Kranke

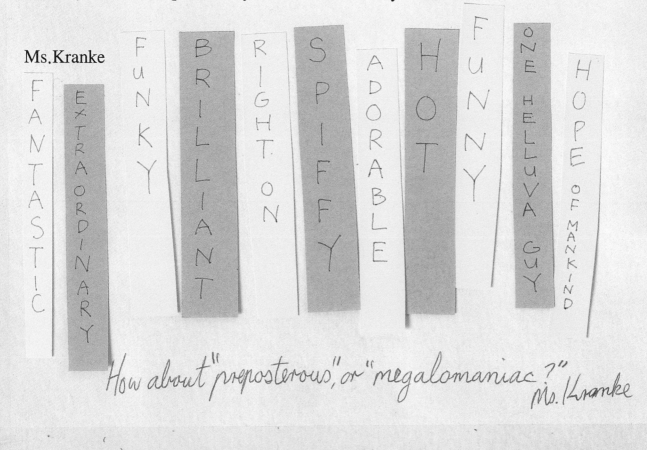

FANTASTIC
EXTRAORDINARY
FUNKY
BRILLIANT
RIGHT ON
SPIFFY
ADORABLE
HOT
FUNNY
ONE HELLUVA GUY
HOPE OF MANKIND

How about "preposterous", or "megalomaniac?"
Ms. Kranke

"Acrostic poem" by Troy Thompson

T otally cool

R ing leader

O wner of two killer dogs

Y et cuddly in his P.J.'s.

T ougher than any other kid

H as genius IQ

O rders three curried pies every big-lunch

M anages to aerate without detection

Not entirely without detection! Ms. K.

P lans to be a cop

S oon to be named Head Prefect

No, I'm not Troy.

O ften mistaken for Jean-Claude Van Damme

N ever been caught with his pants down (except on a school camp)

Thank you, Troy, for stopping your drawing Jat the knees. All I can say is I'm glad I wasn't on that particular camp! 8/10 Ms. Krankee

My Girlfriend Kylie Dragg
by TROY (THE WORLD'S GREATEST LOVER) THOMPSON

Kooky (still likes AC/DC)

Ying-Yang balanced (she Ying-, me Yang)

Liberated (from her Mum and Dad)

Immense (her brain, I mean)

Excellent (cool)

Dad drives a Porsche (red convertible)

Rehabilitated (She used to go to Saint Pauline's)

Agitator (for women's rights)

Greasy (she's got dreadlocks)

Goddess (to me, anyway)

Kooky

Ying-Yang

Liberated

Immense

Excellent

This is not a picture of Kylie, Ms. Kranke, but is based on a picture of a lady I saw in an art book. The snake is based on my visit to the zoo.

You do have a fevered imagination, Troy.

I am very grateful for you putting it in writing that this is *not* a picture of Kylie in any way, shape, or form. But, once again, I am just a bit concerned about what Kylie, or her parents, may make of this. Could you please paint on a shirt and pants and maybe socks and shoes. Please? Ms. Kranke

POETRY ASSIGNMENT XI

We all have a favorite color.   I think that mine is gray. That's certainly the color of my favorite cardigan. For this assignment, try writing a poem about anything and everything that is your favorite color.

Ms. Kranke

Misty Gray
Cool Gray
Dark Gray
Warm Gray
Bright Gray

It's a gray day!

THE COLOR PINK

by Dr Troy (Feel Good) Thompson
(Psychiatric Color Consultant to the Stars)

Some people say that pink is for sissies,

For baby girls and all other missies,

But I don't think that, no not for a minute

Because pink is the color of   Life Be In It

Do I recognize myself in some of these pictures, Troy? I suspect so. But please could you just make it clear I'm wearing a suit here →

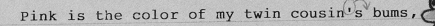

Pink is the color of my twin cousin's bums,

Of dimples on plums,

Of inside our gums,

And strawberry ice cream and other yum yums.

Pink is the color of the sky right on dawn,

Of a well-boiled prawn,

Of the mushroom toad's spawn,

And the color of tonsils before they're withdrawn

(that's just if you yawn)!

I feel I've got off lightly.
No references to my dentures, or bald spot!
Mr. K.

Pink is the color of icing on cakes

(The sugary mouse sort that my mother bakes),

Of some of the nicest of McDonald's shakes

And even the rattles on certain cute snakes.

So for kids who wear black every day and all night

'Cause they think they are Gothic (or some other fright),

Dr Troy

Life Be In It

You should sit up and take notice of Troy Thompson, your shrink,

Looking at your pictures, I'd say pink's the color of sunburn and bruising!

Who says, "Y'only haff livin' if y'ain't wearin' pink".

A fine effort!

But I am glad you looked elsewhere for your "Gothic" reference. I/c Ms. Brazel.

NOTICE TO STUDENTS OF MS. KRANKE'S YEAR 6 CLASS

Here at last is the official application form for the ANNUAL FARMERS' AUXILIARY (INC. BULL BREEDERS' ASSOCIATION) POETRY PRIZE which I want you all to enter. Remember that the winner will receive two prizes: (1) a computer and (2) five hundred dollars worth of software (of the winner's choice) for his or her school. Isn't that EXCITING? So I want you all to fill out the attached form, and submit it to me with your poem. I will pass your entry on to the judges. Good luck to you all and remember our motto: TRY HARDER!

FARMERS' AUXILIARY

(INC. BULL BREEDERS' ASSOCIATION), DAGGABURRA BRANCH

ANNUAL POETRY CONTEST: APPLICATION FORM

This year's contest is for the best free choice poem written by a boy or girl aged between 11 and 13 years at the time of entry. The entrant may write in any poetic style on any topic of his or her choice. Submit all entries (only one per person) to me through your teacher.

Florence Scone-Lammy
Chair, Daggaburra Branch

NAME OF APPLICANT: Troy Thompson   **SEX:** Boy child

AGE: Eleven years three months seven days and one hour

SCHOOL ATTENDED: DAGGABBURRA STATE

TYPE OR FORM OF POEM ENTERED: Sonnet

TITLE OF POEM: My Teacher

INSPIRATION OR REASON FOR WRITING POEM:

My sister Keesha- Louise was doing an assignment for school called "Analyzing teachers in the Movies" so I got to watch some of the videos she was analyzing. There was this one called "The Dead Poets' Society" which sounded cool (like a horror movie) but turned out to be really stupid because Robin Williams, who was the teacher, ripped up this poetry book and Ms. Kranke - my teacher - taught us to respect poetry.

But there was this other movie which was an old black and white one called "To Sir with Love" that sounded really boring but turned out to be OK because this girl called Loo Loo sang this teacher a song that said he had "taken her from crayons to perfume" which meant that he had helped her to grow up.

Well, that's what doing poetry with Ms. Kranke has done for me, but I still like using crayons and I haven't started using perfume yet but I think that Royce - my big brother - does when he goes to clubs to pick up chicks.

So my poem for the contest is about my teacher Ms. Kranke, who looks mean but is probably the best teacher I ever had. Thank you. Troy Thompson.

P.S. Another inspiration for entering the contest was to win the prizes.

Here is my poem for your contest. It is a Shakespearean Sonnet
entitled **MY TEACHER** by Troy Thompson.Dedicated to Ms.Kranke.

Yes it's true that you are very old
And time wasn't kind to you
But sometimes I see you with hair of gold
When you were twenty-two.
And sometimes I feel just a little bit sad
'Cause you had no kids of your own,
But try to remember and try to feel glad
That I'm right there if you would just phone.
And sometimes when you're misty and gray
And your eyes drift away from the light
I imagine you dream of a man far away
Who died with his medals all bright.
But whatever you're thinking, Ms. Kranke, please know
That you taught me, Troy Thompson, to grow.

Portrait of a Winner

New!

200MHz

SNIK

BONK!

SHOOOM!

¡PAF! ¡ZAP!

First American Edition 2003 by
Kane/Miller Book Publishers,Inc.
La Jolla, California

First published in Australia in 1998
by Thomas C. Lothian Pty Ltd
Text copyright © Gary Crew 1998
Illustrations copyright ©Craig Smith 1998

Library of Congress Control Number:
2002117380
Printed and bound in Singapore

1 2 3 4 5 6 7 8 9 10
ISBN 1-929132-52-2

Illustration media: ink, gouache, texta,
collage, pencil and computer generated images.